Alain Dag'Naud

Professor of History

BRITTANY

English edition

Translated by Juan Paolo Perré

**Photography by
Jean-Paul Gisserot**

EDITIONS JEAN-PAUL GISSEROT

2

BRITTANY

On the edge of "terra firma", the islands of Sein and Ouessant, at the tip of Brittany, rest opposite a vast and neverending ocean which was once thought to extend mercilessly to a bottomless void. In Finistère, the three rocky peaks of Raz, Crozon and Saint-Mathieu, are Neptune's trident anchored in the Atlantic. The coast, a rampart of mineral stretching 1,200 meters in length, bristled with points and sprinkled with reefs and inlets opposes the tempestuous waters. In the bays of Mont-Saint-Michel or Trépassés, the sunken cities of Porspican, Ys and Nazado tell of their incessant battle against the waves: Brittany is a land of the ocean.

Brittany is also a land which possesses the hardest of rock: granite, gneiss, sandstone and shale, all a witness to the beginning of the earth's being when fire petrified all. A work carried out, first of all, at the bottom of the oceans' floors. The hercynian fold, with an age of some six hundred million years, gave rise to such powerful montain ranges as l'Amorique, the Massif Central, les Vosges and the Ardennes. In Brittany, erosion left these peaks, in previous times towering four thousand meters, with only those amounting to 384 meters in Tuchenn-ar-Gador, in the Monts d'Arrée. An erosion so powerful that its dug-out base was leveled to its most ancient layers which date back one billion three hundred million years as in the bays of Saint-Brieuc or Léon. The alpine fold of the Tertiary era was too far off to rebuild the Massif Amoricain, but it provoked a series of fractures which give the relief its infinitely varied look.

OF WATER AND FIRE

The brittanic landscapes directly reflect this story which is as old as the world itself. Two rows of summits spreading from east to west form the visible skeleton of the Massif. To the north, the Domnonian mountain range contains Mont d'Arrée and Mont Menez-Bré. To the south, the anticlinal of Cornouaille is capped by the Black Mountains, the marshes of Lanvaux and the furrows of Brittany. Here, the peaks thrashed by the wind and called les roc'h, rise to the surface. Here, the heavy hilltops of the Menez adorned with savage moors, dominate the area. These two crests hold in the Châteaulin basin to the west, and the basin in Rennes to the east, where the hemmed in rivers of the Aulne, Blavet and the Vilaine weave and flow.

The coast, the golden belt of the Armor, displays its highest cliffs on the English Channel. Valleys, inondated for ten thousand years by the rise of the water, gut the coast: Rance, Trieux, les Abers and l'Odet are the most famous of these fjords, or rias which invade the far-reaching land during high tide. Throughout the open space of the water, island jut out of the waves: Cézembre, Bréhat, Batz,

Carnac (Morbihan)

Crozon (Finistère)

Paimpol (Côtes d'Armor)

Ouessant, Sein, Glénan, Groix, Belle-Ile, Honat, Hoedic and so many others. From the Emerald coast-the site of Saint Malo to the Armour coast towards the Loire estuary, passing by the pink Granite coasts and the coasts of Léon, Finistère and Cornouaille, and the finally the Megaliths, where rock, earth and sea intertwine.

No matter where one is in Brittany, even in the heart of Argoat, a land of wood, the ocean is present. Because the ocean winds, which are totally pure, carry the sea air filled with iodine. A perfect example of an ocean climate tempered by the Gulf Stream: the winter are mild, Spring comes early, making the mimosa and eucalyptus (unexpected in these latitudes) come to bloom. Summer is not as scorching as many sun-worshippers would wish, but is

this blissful bronzing which they look for a good thing? It is true that the rain, which is less abundant in Rennes (684 mm per year) than in Nice (810 mm) falls longer and during any season. But a few days of drizzle have never discouraged the true nature-lover. The rain is one of the many charms of Amorica, like the wind which bends the trees and provokes storms when it is northwesterly or southwesterly. Nothing so small could upset a Breton. A nice oilskin, a marine's sweater and all is ready.

With such a climate, Brittany is a haven for an incredibly rich wildlife. While meandering around Ellez, you will perhaps discover a beaver's hut or a badger's trail. A little further a couple of otters frolic. In the Menez-Meur park, wolves, deer and auroch roam.

Birds by the thousand, make their rendez-vous on Ouessant island, the Sept-Iles (Seven Islands) or on the cliffs of Fréhel: cinder herons, gulls and seagulls...the sylvette parula and the guiraca with its rose-colored chest come from North America, the stonechat which left its home in Africa, the boreal warbler abandonned Siberia. Alongside the road, void of trees, the enclosures of hedges hide a variety of species, birds, butterflies, bumblebees...

Lanleff (Côtes d'Armor)

The Breton earth appears to be of poor quality. Some grains on Ile-et-Vilaine, fodder for beasts (Brittany is one of the largest regions for the breeding of pigs and milk cows), and especially land cultivated by market gardeners on the coastal plains, with new potatoes, the famous artichokes and cauliflower from Léon and Trégorrois, peas and green beans from Morbihan, strawberries from Plougastel-Daoulas...But if you take the time to look a little closer, you will discover a botanical treasure which is as varied as it is discrete. Moors of broom, gorse and heather, fields of blue molinie spotted with orchids, pinguicules scattered throughout the moss, bindweed and thistle nestled into the crevices of coastal rocks and maritime cabbage from the beaches of fine sand. The large forests which existed before have not survived except for the scattered forests in Heulgoat, Quénécan, Grandchamp, Loudéac and

Suscinio (Morbihan)

Paimpont and the ancient Brocéliande. But the oak and beech with underbrush strewn with anemone and and hyacinth are especially beautiful.

THE LAND OF MEGALITHS

An old country swept by the sea sprays, Brittany has achieved an extraordinary alchemy. Those people who have let themselves be struck by its charm, who drank once the potions of its sacred

fountains are never released from its spell. The people who came in waves to establish themselves in Amorica since the beginning have all experienced this. Very early on, they worshipped the sun whose fires set in the west on the ocean's waves. They made this land an immense holy place, the last stop for the deceased before the parting of their souls to the hereafter.

Thus, the explanation of the imposing temples and the formidable tombs of stone built here seven millennium ago, two thousand years before the Pyramids of Egypt.

An uncountable number of megaliths pierce the earth in Brittany. What is their message? How could they have been erected? Some exceed three hundred tons in weight. There are as many mysteries as the unconditional scientific minds elude by simple arguments: rolling of blocks on

round stones, lifting by a system of cords, beams, or a massive usage of manpower. The function of these megaliths depend on their form.

Menhirs are enormouns blocks driven vertically into certain specific places. It could be said that they are positioned above the convergence points of the telluric waves, acupuncture points on the energy lines of the Earth. When the menhirs are grouped in lines on the vast sacred land, like in Carnac, in Lagatjar or in Saint-Just they are called alignments. Their orientation from east to west leads one to

*La Roche aux Fées
(Ille et Vilaine)*

believe that they were consacrated for a solar cult or worship. But they layout plans much more complicated on the Amorican grounds, sometimes circles or

Languidou (Finistère)

cromlechs, which corresponded to the magnetic spectrum of this ancient massive structure which was periodically shaken by sismic tremors. The menhirs regulated these deep forces.

Dolmens are the funeral chambers composed of vertical blocks supporting a covering table. They were buried in a tumulus of earth or loose stones, which amounted to being a cairn, often sheltering several dolmens or even covered alleyways, long corridors of erected stones. From Saint Michel to Carnac, Barnenez and Gavrinis

Irvillac (Finistère)

one can see remarkable examples of this work. The first ones measure 120 meters in length and 12 meters in height: the one in Barnenez, dating back to 4700 BC, contained eleven dolmens with corridors! In their mounds, the dead were honored and above all, their spirits evoked.

THE GAULS OF ASTERIX

From the Bronze age to the Iron age, from one thousand to the first century before our time, the Celts who came from the borders of the Rhine and the Danube, established themselves throughout Gaul and went as far as the Iberian Galicia, in Scotland and in Ireland. After having pushed the indigenous people of the Stone Age back, five celtic tribes dominated Amorica: the Vénètes in Vannes, the

Osismes in north Finistère, the Curiosolites of Corseul, toward the northern coast, the Diablintes of Doe, on the Mont Saint Michel bay, the Rhedones in Condate (Rennes), and the Namnètes in Nantes. These Gauls were "barbarians" lead by a warlike and troublesome aristocrat and religious leaders, the druids, magi, dominators of the elements, soothsayers and sacrificers, worshippers of the oak and mistletoe. On the feast of Samain, the first of November, the barley beer ran like water. The fire from the inferno, or tantad, and the sharing of a ritual meal sealed the union between the warriors inside each clan. Agriculture improved with the help of the iron swing plough, artisinal work was in the midst of great expansion (ceramics, jewelry, tools...), and business developed. Situated at the heart of maritime routes of the Atlantic, the peninsula became a required passage point. With the pewter of Cornouaille and the argentiferous lead of the local

Guimiliau (Finistère)

Page to right:

Upper : Guimiliau (Finistère)

Lower : Trémazan (Finistère)

Concarneau (Finistère)

mines, they created money: a means of exchange and a symbol of opulence.

At the time of the war of the Gauls, Julius Cesar coveted this strategically important province. Starting from 56 B.C. he battled against the Vénètes in a naval battle around the Mobihan. The heavy celtic ships were destroyed by the imperial galley opposite Port Navalo. All of Amorica submits and becomes romanized, except of course a small village inhabited by steadfast gauls, but that's another story...

THE TIME OF THE FRIARS

Amorica doesn't become Brittany until the Vth century, with the arrival of the Celts delegated from accross the Channel by the Anglos and the Saxons. One after the other, the british villages are deserted. Their inhabitants take to the sea guided by their religious leaders, most often friars. They regroup their original villages in Amorica, form new parishes, and start the christianization the population. This vast migration was the object of many a marvellous account: Malo and his 65 companions are mysteriously guided across the waves; the gaul Brieuc strikes down the devil who wants to prevent his boat from advancing; the friar Pol kills a dragon; Tudgdual, who came from Devon, leaves with his family and 72 friends at the command of an angel ("Tudgdual, God commands you to leave Great Britain and to go without haste to the small Britain"); others cross the sea atop large wheels of stone!

All of these adventurous friars,

Menez Bré (Côtes d'Armor)

Saint-Avé - Notre-Dame du Loc (Morbihan)

Tumiac - tumulus (Morbihan)

Daoulas (Finistère)

voted, including the woman. On the day of the annual assembly, a pilgramage, the Pardon, was organized in honor of the founding friar who had become the patron saint of the village. The sacred path lead from the church and stopped near one of the many sacred fountains, always miraculous, which adorn Brittany: Notre Dame de Lorette in Saint Guen, Le Guiaudet in Lanrivain, Larré, Saint Julitte in Ambon, Saint Uriac in Corseul... The most beautiful Pardons today are those in Folgoët, Josselin, Saint Jean Trolimon, Rumengol, which are all in honor of Our Lady, the one in Plonevez-Porzay in hommage of Saint Anne la Palud, the one in Locronan for Saint Ronan, and the one in Tréguier in honor of Saint Yves, the breton judge of the XIIIth century who became the advocate of the poor and was canonized shortly after his death, and to whos credit owe numerous miracles.

Seven bishops assure the unity of all of the parishes: Dol, founded by Saint Samson, Tréguier lead by Tugdual, Quimper, the base of Corentin, Vannes, with Saint Patern, Saint Pol de Léon, Saint Brieuc and Saint Malo. Until the XIXth century, the Bretons paid hommage to these founding saints by doing, at least once in their lives, the Tro Breiz, a jaunt around the foot of Brittany by the seven cathedrals; a pilgrimage which was 530 kilometers in length.

often Irish, endowed with magical powers inherited from druids, became saints. In their names, Brittany is sprinkled with chapels in granite. Each clan, each family in the largest sense of the word, gathered at their sanctuary. This is the origin of the brotherhoods which would mark the history of each village in Brittany. They all united inside of the sacred place at the ringing of the bell. Everyone

Ile-Grande (Côtes d'Armor)

TWO LANGUAGES

It was these missionaries from across the Channel who brought the name of Brittany to Amorica which we see appear only since the VIth century in the writings of Grégoire de Tours and de Fortunat. They also brought back a vitality to the Amorican language, a relation to ancient Celtic spoken perhaps from the Xth century B.C. Breton belongs to the so-called british family, which includes also Gallic and Cornic (in Cornouaille).

This language, enriched by the eventual borrowings from Latin and roman dielects from the west of France, possesses a rich vocabulary and an extremely flexible grammar. The following texts from the end of the Middle Ages bear witness to this: *La Vie de sainte Nonne* and the poem intitled, *Le Mirouer de la Mort*, which has a length of 3 602 verses. Many verbs and very few adjectives, words could be infinitely combined to form new ones.

Cast -Saint-Hubert (Finistère)

Unfortunately, in the XIXth century, public school and its zealous teachers brought on the eradication of this provincial language because it was only spoken by country people. Bretons eventually wound up with no knowledge as to how their language was written. Today, it's the intellectuals who have been carrying the flame in support. They have revealed that the language is an instrument of expressive poetry. At the very most, they forced themselves to simplify the grammar to adapt to contemporary thought. In the breton universities, posts for the study of celtic have been created. In Brest, for example, but also in Rennes,

Paimpont (Ille et Vilaine)

capital of Upper Brittany where breton was not spoken. Because Brittany was bilingual: only west of the path of Saint Brieuc-Vannes was Breton-speaking. To the east, gallic was spoken, that is, French.

GRAIL AND CHIVALRY

Another paradox (Brittany is full of them), is the apparition of the famous "breton books" in the country of the French language. These were the written version of the celtic legends sung by the bards. A late christianization, the remains of paganism, the tradition of the celtic clans so well adapted to the chivalry, and above all the strong magical power of the province explained the mysterious and enchanting atmosphere which these accounts were bathed in. The innumerable celtic gods, Bel, le solaire, Gargantua, Anna the earth

Brasparts (Finistère)

mother, Morgane who guards over the waters, the facetious korrigans, blacksmith dwarfs of the underground dens, Marc'h the horse god, Arzur the bear and the Envel twins are the occult heros of Armorica. One finds their marks in the adventures of the Knights of the Round Table and the love story of Tristan and Isolde.

King Arthur, overlord of the Knights of the Round Table, identified with Arzur the bear king, undoubtably took after a military chief of the Bretons in his heroic adventures against the Saxons from across the Channel around the year 500. The souvenirs of his prowess have inspired many writers, Geoffrey de Monmouth, Wace, Chrétien de Troyes...who say in him the ideal king, a model of knightly virtues. His ships want by the famous names of Perceval, Lancelot, and Gauvain, all proud lords in search of the Grail, this vase which was used at the Last Supper and in which Joseph of Arymathia gathered the liquid of life which flowed from the body of Christ. A neverending conquest where the true behind everyone was revealed. Arthur carries out his last combat in England, in Salisbury. Wounded, he gives the order to plunge his sword, the Excaliber, into the lake nearby. An arm springs from the water, takes the sword and disappears. A vessel berths. Arthur sees his dead sister and several fairies who accompany her. They leave and disappear forever. Three days later, his burial place is found in the Black Chapel.

Nantes (Loire Atlantique)

Malestroit (Morbihan)

Quimper (Finistère)

Dinan (Côtes d'Armor)

The Tristan cycle also had great success in the Middle Ages. The orphan son of a Cornouaille lord in Amorica, Tristan was brought up by his uncle, king Marc. King Marc has the young man go on a quest across the Channel for his future spouse, the beautiful Isolde, the daughter of the king of Ireland. The princess and the emissary sail towards Armorica in the company of the faithful Brangien, lady's companion, who carries a love potion for the future lovers. But by error, on the ship, Isolde and Tristan drink the magic potion. They love each other and after becoming queen, Isolde never stops seeing Tristan. Denounced, condemned, chased after and finally pardonned, the two young lovers separate so that they no longer betray Marc. Tristan marries another Isolde, aux Blanche-Mains, daughter of the Duke of Nantes. But when he is wounded, he has Isolde the Blonde searched for for she alone can cure him. If she accepts to come to him, the sail will be white and black in the opposite case. Isolde aux Blanche-Mains discovers his secret. When the vessel carrying her rival approaches, she tells Tristan that the sail is black. Tristan dies and Isolde, arriving too late collapses and dies in his arms. Marc pardons them once again and buries them side by side one another. These accounts where the heros cross from one bank of the Channel to the other tells of the intensity between the bonds which unify Great Britain with the Small Britain. They mark also the persistance of the celtic roots. The heart of these legends, the famous forest of Brocéliande, near Paimpont, preserves in its toponomy, the souvenir of its magical past: the prophet Merlin meets the fairy Viviane at the fountain of Barenton. Near the wonderful source, with which a few drops can unleash a storm, Yvain, the knight of the Lion, rids the country of the black knight. Lancelot was brought up by Viviane at the bottom of the lake of

Carhaix (Finistère)

Saint-Herbot (Finistère)

Saint-Thégonnec (Finistère)

Dol (Ille et Vilaine)

Diana. Later, he vows his love for the queen Gwenevier on the Secret bridge. In the Valley with no Return, Morgan the magician is skilled in all sciences. In a clearing, one can still see the magic circle, hyaline citadel, wherein Viviane locked Merlin, her consenting lover. A simple rock marks this tomb.

The coast is also a place of mysteries. The most famous is the sinking of the city of Ys at the Finistère point. In the year 421, King Gradlon, master of Amorica, was proud of his victories against the barbaric hourdes, proud of his capital, Ys the opulent city, protected from the fury of the Atlantic by enormous dykes, Les Portes de la Mer (Gates to the Sea). He was even prouder of his beautiful daughter Dahud, who drew her tired lovers into the shifting sand. One night, Dahud steals the golden key to the locks and unleashes the seas onto the city. Saint Guénolé intervenes to save Gradlon, but the princess drowns in the Pertuis de Dahut. The day after, the sea is calm. Ys had disappeared.

"When Paris drowns

Ys will be reborn", a saying predicts.

THE DUCHESS OF BRITTANY

A clearly noted history begins with the end of the clans and the unifying politics lead by Charlemagne and his successors. In 825, Louis le Pieux, son of the emperor, hands over the government of the province erected as a dukedom to Nominoé. Nominoé rebels in 841. On November 21, 845, by the victory of Ballon against Charles le Chauve, son of Louis le Pieux, he liberates Brittany from suzerainty.

Redon (Ille et Vilaine)

The decades which follow are marked by the ravage by the Normands. Defeated in 888 at Questembert by Alain Ist the Great, they wouldn't stop their raids until 939, under the reign of the Duke Alain Barbe-Torte. Meanwhile, Brittany is covered with fortresses destined to resist pillages. But the lords who command them, true despots in love with war, exploit the country people, contest the power of the dukedom and alley themselves with the houses of Nantes and Rennes. It is anarchy. In 1158, Henri II Plantagenêt, count of Anjou, duke of Aquitaine and Normandy, King of England, take advantage of this to invade the peninsula and impose his son Geoffroy in replacement of Conan IV. Brittany next falls under the supervision of the Capetians after the marriage of Allix of Brittany with Pierre of Dreux (1213).

Pontcroix (Finistère)

Coveted by France and England, Brittany is at the heart of one of the major episodes of the Hundred Year war. In 1341, the reigning duke, Jean III, dies without a direct heir. Two substitutes are in line: his half-brother Jean de Montfort, close to the English, and his niece Jeanne de Penthièvre, wife of Charles de Blois, nephew of the King of France. Jeanne is designated as the sole heir by a decree of the King of France. (September 7, 1341). Jean de Montfort rebels and assures himself the support of Edward III of England. The war of Succession begins. It would last 23 years. Montfort and Penthièvre, English and French are hand in hand, conqueror and conquered. When the lords are taken prisoner, their wives take over the torch. Between Jeanne de Penthièvre and Jeanne

Pontivy (Morbihan)

Largoët-Elven (Morbihan)

de Flandre, wife of Montfort, it is hatred until death. Battles and duels insue. In March 1351, Robert de Beaumanoir, captain of Josselin, provokes the garrison of Ploërmel, favored by Montfort. Thirty knights of each side come face to face. At night, the franco-bretons are declared victorious with "only" six deaths against the others' nine.

In 1364, Jeanne de Penthièvre urges her husband Charles de Blois to attack Jean de Montfort at Auray. Charles is killed: the fine flower of the breton knighthood is dead. On April 12, 1365, the treaty of Guérande takes care of the succession: the Montforts are declared legitimate heirs but if there is no male heir then Brittany would pass into the hands of the Penthièvres.

Josselin (Morbihan)

The real winners are the country people, ruined by the rides of the roadmen, lords-crooks, made thirsty by blunders, exhausted by the famines, desecrated by the black plaque from 1348-49. This war didn't have only negative effects. It highlighted strong personalities like Charles de Blois, elevated to the rank of the saints and especially Bertrand du Guesclin who pursued his combats under the banner of the King of France and became captain of the Great Companies, duke of Trastamare of Spain, King of Grenada, then constable of France, chief of the royal armies before dying in Auvergne at the beginning of May 1380. This war above all reassured the Montforts who created a chamber of accounts and make the Parliment of Brittany a sovereign court in 1485. The good

Saint-Malo (Ille et Vilaine)

Saint-Thégonnec (Finistère)

relations of this dynasty with the house of England allowed the province to play out its role of maritime power without problem. It was a nearly unescapeable point on the commercial route between Spain, Bordeaux and England.

THE DUCHESS ANNE

When Louis XI died in 1483, François II of Brittany intended to take advantage of the vacancy in the Monarchy to totally dislodge Brittany from the supervision of its strong neighbor. He encounters problems. On July 28, 1488, the french army win the battle of Saint Aubain du Cormier. On August 20, François II must sign the unfortunate treaty of Verger which imposes on him the hommage-liege to the King of France and forbids him from marrying his two daughters, Anne and Isabelle, without prior consent from the King. François does not survive this humiliation. He leaves as heir a twelve year old infant, Anne, the orphan, fragile and lame, neglected of everything but with a rare courage. In spite of the opposition from a portion of the breton nobility, Anne is crowned Duchess of Brittany in Rennes. Then she chooses to marry Maximilian de Habsbourg, chief of the Holy Roman-German Empire. France equally invades Brittany. Nantes and Rennes are occupied. Charles VIII obtains the annulation of the marriage of Anne with Maximilian from the Pope and marries the duchess on December 6, 1491 in Langeais.

Widow at 21 years old, Anne retakes hold of the soveriegn rights to Brittany. Louis XII, heir to the kingdom of France, annuls his own marriage in order to marry the one he called "little Brette" in Nantes on January 8, 1499. Anne reserved the right to hand over the position of duchess to her heirs, and insists that taxes not be raised nor soldiers be removed without the accord of the states of Brittany. From this marriage, are born four children, two sons who die at an early age, and two daughters, Claude and Renée. Skillfully, Louis XII organizes the marriage of Claude with the heir to the throne, the future François Ist. Anne dies in 1514, Louis in 1515. Claude inherits the dukedom which will lead to the throne of France. The union is ratified by the parliment of Vannes in 1532.

The duchess Anne is so popular in Brittany that numerous infants receive her first name at baptism. The cult of saint Anne, the grandmother of Christ is confirmed. In 1623, Yves Nicolagic, farmer in Ker-Anna, near Auray, sees on several occasions his house light up. Near the source where he brought his cows to drink, a strange woman appeared on July 25, 1624. "Yves Nicolazic, do not be afraid, I am Anne, mother of Marie. Tell your rector that there was a chapel here before that was dedicated to me. 924 years have passed since its ruin. I want it to be rebuilt as fast as possible and for you to take care of this." On the night of March 8 to 9, 1625, excavations reveal an old statue in wood of saint Anne. A sanctuary is built. It is today the largest in Brittany. "Dead or alive, every Breton must obey saint Anne."

Saint-Thégonnec (Finistère)

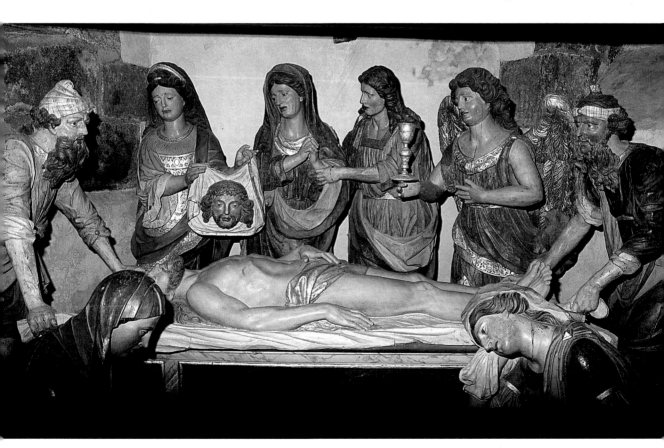

Rumengol (Finistère)

The textile craft industry enlivened numerous internal villages which display their opulence by creating exhuberant religious monuments, the parish walls, Guimilian, Plougastel-Daoulas, Pleyben, Tronoën, Sizun, Saint-Thégonnec are the most celebrated enclosures of this Baroque Renaissance, a meeting place for the living and the dead, where the fascination with death was expressed, l'Ankou, omnipresent in the breton soul. These sacred fields present related layouts. Past the triumphal arch, there is a church, an ossuary and especially a sculpted calvary with many personnages from the Christ Passion depicted.

The Bretons are above all a sea people. It is the sea which has made their fame and their fortune. Born is Saint Malo in 1494, Jacques Cartier explored the northern coasts of America, goes back to the Saint Laurent, discovers tobacco and allows France to implant itself in Canada.

The sea is also the kingdom of the privateers who terrorize the English on all seas. Because the people of "business" on the seas do well as pirates. They are people of the king and all the better if they improve their interests. Saint Malo, Paimpol, Morlaix, Roscoff, Brest, Port Louis, Lorient, Le Croisic and Nantes are the adventurer's snags, ready for anything, for any problems regardless of how crazed or out of control. Starting 1512, Hervé de Portzmoquer, dit Primanguet, commander of the Cordelière, takes on the English at Saint Matthew. Duguay-Trouin, a Saint Malo resident leaves for the first time in 1679. He was sixteen. He became commander at eighteen. Later he is near Brazil, attacking the portuguese ships carrying silver. He forces through the harbor of Rio and siezes hold of the city which is looted. Jacques Cassard, originally from Nantes, battles in the Antilles in the year 1710 and ravages the dutch colony

DISCOVERERS, PRIVATEERS AND THE PEOPLE OF TERRE NEUVE

Between the XVIth and XVIIIth centuries, Brittany experience a relative prosperity which hinged on four activities: work with hemp or flax tile, sea "business", the dealing of Africans and the fishing of cod on the banks of Terre Neuve.

no scruples. Four hundred thousand Africans are inhumanly and savagely kidnapped over one hundred years by these traffikers.

Fishing at Terre Neuve, around Canada, was the livelihood of several thousand marines until the beginning of the XXth century. A dramatic epic: the people of Terre Neuve, each year, were up against months of battling against the perils of the sea, often until death. When the brick-schooner or the three-masts leave Saint Malo in the Spring, it is a depart to the unknown. The women knew it well; they mourned until their return. The crossing lasted four weeks, fishing on the banks prolonged oneself six months. The thirty equipment men of the sailing ship feared the fog, a cause of many accidents, and the storms which pushed them further from the dories, these small boats from where the line is tended. They suffered from the cold, malnutrician, and always the same soup of cod heads with a glass of alcohol, sickness, uncomfortable beds niched against the hull. But these convicts of the ocean were well-paid, three times the balance in the Royale and when they entered port from August to the end of October, they could cultivate the earth, because most were also farmers. Certain ships were reported missing. The widows never stopped their mourning. It was once said that Brittany was a country of women in black.

Plougastel (Finistère)

on Surinam. After each expedition, he went back to Saint Malo with several boats taken from the enemy in tow. But unaccustomed as he was with the manners of the court, he injures a minister at Versailles and finishes the rest of his days in prison at Fort Ham.

The four Surcouf brothers from Malo are known for their exploits against the English in the Indian Ocean between 1789 and 1809. Robert Surcouf is particularly famous for his intrepitude. In 1798-99, at the head of the ship *La Clarisse*, armed only with fourteen canons, he successively captures two english ships loaded with pepper, a danish ship, a portuguese, an american...With *La Confiance*, he plans an assult on the famous english vessel, *Kent*, which has 400 men and 38 canons aboard. Contrary to Cassard, Robert Surcouf becomes one of the richest shipowners of France.

The triangular business of slaves between Amorica, equitorial Africa and America, creates a fortune for a few shipowners of Nantes with

Pointe Saint-Mathieu
(Finistère)

Fougères (Ille et Vilaine)

THE REBELLIOUS

Those who live with the Ankou, who confront the seas, cannot fear the human laws. "Better to die than to be dishonored" "Potius mori quam foedari", this was what was read on the patch on the ermine blazers worn by the Breton dukes. The Bretons have always been and will be revolters. In 1588, they revolted against the governor, duke of Mercoeur; in 1675, against the tax on stamped paper; in 1718, at the side of the young marquis of Pontcallec. We pretend that the Bretons are in love with orders and very conservative. Nothing could be more false. with the propulsion of chouanism there were quite vicious conter-revolutions. To forget that the Revolution came from Brittany. Starting from 1764, the Parliment of Rennes and its general prosecutor La Chalotais contest the royal authority represented by the govenor of Aiguillon. In 1789, the 66 breton deputies of the Third State and of the lower clergy organize themselves into a group at Versailles, the future "Breton Club" which would become the "Jacobins Club", and would play a propulsive role in the popular demands. Le Chapelier, chief of the breton club, is elected president of the National Assembly formed the 3 August 1789. The next day, during the night, the privileges are abolished.

Therefore, why the abrupt change which lead in chouanism? Because of a worry of independance and liberty. The suppression of the French provinces and their transformation into departments crosses Brittany off the administrative map. On July 12,

Saint-Malo (Ille et Vilaine)

1790, the civil Constitution of the clergy imposes election by the people for the heads of the religious bodies and eliminates four breton bishops in order to harmonize the diosceses with the new departments. This was to touch the clan roots of celtism and the deep mysticism of every Breton. Contrary to the Vendéeians who proclaimed "God and my king", the Chouans had for slogan "God and my country".

Chouanism broke out mid-March 1793, when the centralised State wants to impose a mass lifting of conscripts, without prior agreement from breton authorities. The insurrection is prolonged until the Concordat of July 1801. It is punctuated with atrocities like the 4,800 drownings of Nantes carried out by the conventional Carrier in October 1893, or the execution of emmigrants who debarked at Quiberon on June 27 1795: for two months, twelve men were shot each day on the Champ des Martyrs (Field of Martyrs) in Auray.

The most famous chouan chief is without a doubt, Cadoudal. Born in Kerléano, near Auray, in 1771, this son of a rich farmer multiplied the efforts against the blue republicans, then the effort against Bonaparte. Suspected of being the instigator for the attack of the infernal machine of the 3rd of Nivôse then an attempt to kidnap the Prime consulate, Georges Cadoudal is stopped in Paris on March 9, 1804. He refuses to seek his pardon and is executed June 25.

Brittany comes out of the Revolution and the Empire

Saint-Malo (Ille et Vilaine)

Saint-Malo (Ille et Vilaine)

Pontrieux (Côtes d'Armor)

weakened: 80,000 chouan soldiers have been killed, tens of thousands of civilians are massacred. Maritime business is ruined by the loss of overseas positions, the defeat of the war marines and the continental blockade. Because of insufficient resources, the Bretons emmigrate by the millions, become missionaries or settlers in the four corners of the earth, enlist in the army, establish themselves in Paris and in the French metropolitan areas. The withdrawal from agriculture and fishing gives Brittany the outdated image of a country of "country bumpkins", ignoring the industrial revolutions, refusing the Ferry school, but sending their children to die first in the trenches of la Somme or Verdun. This is the time of Bécassine.

ABOVE ALL BRETON

A few lightning-swift destinies mark heavily the breton diaspora. François-René de Chateaubriand, born in 1768 at the feodal chateau of Combourg, near Dol, spends his adolescence on the land haunted by the "murmur of the wind" and "seeded with druid stones". The father of Romanticism, engaging politics, one after another Ambassador of Berlin, Minister of Foreign Affairs and Ambassador to Rome, at his death, he leaves a considerable opus: the *Mémoires d'outre-tombe, Atala, René, the Génie du Christianisme*...Very attached to Brittany, he has himself buried around Saint Malo, on the small island of Grand-Bé, facing the ocean.

Landerneau (Finistère)

Vannes (Morbihan)

Locronan (Finistère)

Le Faouët-Sainte-Barbe (Morbihan)

A native of Quimper, René-Théophile Laënnec (1781-1826) practices medecine at the Hôtel-Dieu of Paris where he invents the stethescope which facilitates the listening of pulmonary movement. Constantly on the verge of consumption, he catches the disease and retires to his manor in Kerlouarnec in Ploaré, near Douarnenez, where he dies in 1826.

Lamennais (1782-1854) is the son of a shipowner from Saint Malo. He becomes a priest and denounces the collusion between the church and the monarchy. His manor house in La Chesnaie, in the forest of Coëtquen near Dinan, which became the high-place of liberal catholisme. But the audacious social projects of Lamennais causes him to be condemned by Pope Gregory XVI.

Liscuis-Laniscat
(Côtes d'Armor)

Barnenez (Finistère)

Pointe du Raz (Finistère)

Penmarc'h (Finistère)

Ernest Renan is also a protester. Son of a captain who drowned near Erquy, Renan spends his infancy in Tréguier. He does his studies in Paris, in the seminary directed by Msgr. Dupanloup. But he has doubts. In 1845, he renounces the priesthood. He becomes a professor at the College of France in 1862 and creates a scandal for presenting Christ as "an incomparable man". The next year, he publishes *La Vie de Jésus* which refuses the divine character of Christ.

The Cancal Jeanne Jugan, daughter of a marine-fisher who disappeared at sea, serves as chef's helper at the viscounts of La Choüe, then as guardian for the sick in a hospital before being company lady in Saint Servan. One night in the winter of 1839, she welcomes an old sick woman into the hospital who has neither roof nor resources. Then she houses other sick people. From 1845, she takes care of sixty old persons, men and women, and a few children. To feed them, twice a day she would go from door to door to collect the remains of meals and offerings. Friends help "the great Jeanne". The Little Sisters of the Poor are born. At the death of Jeanne on August 29, 1879, these little sisters known throughout France took care of twenty thousand aged persons!

It is understandable, Bretons are people of character!

The contempt of the "nation" towards its western appendage only upset the isolation of the Bretons and their sense of revolt. In 1898, the Union of breton regionalists, the URB, is created. The National Breton party is founded in 1911. In 1930, the Breton autonomist party presents candidates to the legislature of Guingamp and Rennes. In 1932, the clandestine organization "Gwen ha Du" throws out the monument

Lampaul-Guimiliau (Finistère)

of Rennes symbolizing the union of Brittany and France. In black and white, the breton flag which was created in this era, contained the mystic and dynastic origins of the province: nine horizontal bands which represented the bishops, five black ones for the french language, four white ones for the breton-language bishops. Ermine tails symbolized the dukedom line.

Revolt again during the Second World War, when the Germans invade then occupy the country. If the chiefs of the national breton party, Mordrel and Debauvais, arranged themselves alongside the nazis in the hope of forming an independant Breton state, a satellite of the Reich, it would be a rare Breton who would follow. On June 24, 1940, on the Sein island, the woman clothed in black and wearing their hair in the style of a widow, accompany their husbands and sons, 124 men where the youngest was thirteen years old, to the embarkments which would take them to England where they would continue the coast combats of General deGaulle. At the Liberation, the island and all of its inhabitants receive the Cross of the Resistance. A monument recalls this distinguished fact and bears the inscription in breton: "Kentoc'h Mervel", "Better to die".

In 1940, Brittany becomes a strategic stake for Germany and England. The first ones put up remarkable protected military posts. They have great submarine bases built by requisitioned manpower at Lorient and Brest. The aerodromes of the northern coast are arranged to allow german planes to bomb England. On August 13, 1942, Hitler decides to raise the wall of the Atlantic which Brittany is a main piece. The Todt organization loads the cliffs of fortifications and blockhouses which defend the western access to Europe.

Pleyben (Finistère)

Le Faouët   Adam   (Morbihan)

Saint-Thégonnec   (Finistère)

Le Folgoët (Finistère)

With the help of local resistence, England debark or parachute numerous agents from free France and the Intelligence Service. The network Par O'Leary, Oaktree, Mithridate, Shelburne, take care of evacuating struck-down aviators to England. Finally, the Resistance forms the Saint Marcel underground, in Morbihan, to disorganize the german movements on the day before the allied embarkment at Normandy. A very important stake, Brittany pays a heavy price in the conflict: Nantes, Saint-Malo, Brest, Lorient, Saint-Nazaire are for the most part destroyed by the bombardments and the sieges.

TO THE COUNTRY OF THE SEA

Today, it is still the sea where Brittany gathers a large part of its essential resources. Its fishing ports dot the length of its shores: Lorient and Concarneau are the most active, Camaret and Douarnenez specialize in lobster, Saint-Malo always fish cod, the bassins of Guilvinec, Saint-Guénolé, Loctudy, and Quiberon welcome some of the three thousand multicolor boats which fly the breton flag. Sole, turbot, rays, gilt-head, mackerel, crustaceans are emptied onto the ports daily. With ten thousand

Menhir Saint-Uzec
(Côtes d'Armor)

Quilinen (Finistère)

Kerfons (Côtes d'Armor)

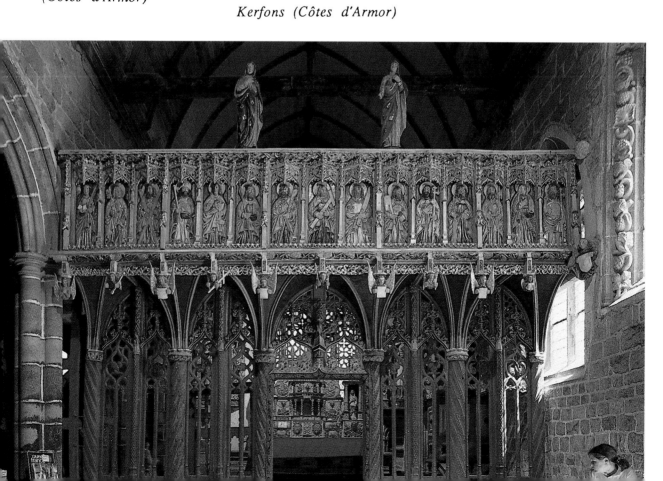

Sizun (Finistère)

Sizun (Finistère)

marines, Brittany surpasses countries which are known for their marines such as Denmark or the Netherlands. Six thousand persons cultivate oysters, muscles and coquilles St-Jacques. The oyster culture flourishes in Cancale, Belon, Morlaix. Everywhere one can gather shells of all types. The sea pushes to the coast the precious wrack which local businesses transform into fertilizer.

The privateer vocation exists also: the arsenals in Brest and Lorient construct most of the french combat vessels. In deep water and

*Lampaul-Guimiliau
(Finistère)*

Paimpol (Côtes d'Armor)

well-protected, the Brest harbor plays a strategic role of the utmost importance in the defense of the Atlantic. Aircraft carriers, battleships and cruisers abode in the war port, the Longue island shelters the Strategic Ocean Force's nuclear submarines. The naval school, a reservoir for marine officers, is set up in Lanvéoc-Poulmic, near Brest. Immense "forms" serve for the naval construction and reparations. In the maritime field, the Bretons are up-to-date in terms of technology: the Oceanological Center of Brittany is in Saint Anne du Portzic, the EPSHOM takes care of marine cartography, the

50

IFREMER interests lie in exploiting mineral and living resources in the seas, as well as fighting against pollution. The last resource of the ocean, tourism is prosperous on these coasts. But do not look for the large tourist complexes. Among the most famous stations of La Baule and Dinard, with their calm and charm, Amorica is privileged for its secret spots for lovers of solitude, the small ports of pleasure where amateurs of sailing can exercise their pleasure as well as the centers for marine rest/relaxation and sea water therapy, benefiting from the riches that the ocean has to offer.

Tourists are more numerous during the large holidays like the ones for terre-neuvas in Paimpol around mid-July, or the one for old rigging in August at Douarnenez.

FROM EARTHENWARE TO THE MINITEL

Adventurers and marginals, isolated on their peninsula, the Bretons have stayed in the background of large industry. Citroën in Rennes, Michelin in Vannes, Thomson CSF in Brest, the refineries of Donges and of course the naval constructions in the ports are not enough to create an industrial force. The older activities with furnishings, shoes regress. Pottery has a place apart. Since 1960, the founding date by Jean-Baptiste Bousquet of the first Quimper manufacturers, the blue and yellow earthenware, utility or decoration, they were created in a specificallt breton style and always appreciated.

Page to right:

Upper:

Brest (Finistère)
Lower:
Saint-Malo (Ille et Vilaine)

Cancale (Ille et Vilaine)

Golfe du Morbihan
(Morbihan)

The most dynamic enterprises are in commerce and agriculture. Bridel and Entremont for dairy products, Guyomarc'h for poultry, UNICOPA, cookies and bisquits, Saupiquet preserves have presented themselves on the marketplace worldwide. The LeClercs of Landerneau, the Rallye group in Brest and Intermarché have given a vigor back to large distribution. La Brioche dorée is implanted everywhere in France.

The cosmetic products of Yves Rocher, in La Gacilly, there is a numerous and faithful clientele. Some enterprises even rank worldwide in their specialty: Bolloré Technology for its polypropylene films, Bétina for their genetic work with farm turkeys, Doux for exporting chicken...Bretons love to innovate: the Minitel was born at the CNET in Lannion and at the Center for the study of telediffusion and

telecommunications in Rennes, which is currently preparing the telephone of the year 2000. Under the curiousity of Pleumeur-Bodou, specialists of the National Center for Telecommunications Studies are listening to satellites. The Ouest-France group possesses very modern installations for printing the highest number of daily french papers and journals.

Brière (Loire-Atlantique)

Lanrigan (Ille et Vilaine)

LIGHTHOUSES AND MANORS

Mixing tradition and the avante-garde, while often forgetting the present, Brittany is surprising. One hardly finds any industrial zones but some cities and villages are surrounded by hideous supermarkets. A concession to "modernism"? There is no pollution here from factories but the ground water is often corrupted by abusive use of nitrates.

Agriculture has remained the domain of small owners, just now being organized into cooperatives, but the restructuring has created problems, which in part has destroyed the wonderful preservation which makes the charm of the country.

Nevertheless. Brittany is and remains the best preserved french province; the most authentic and the most attractive. How can one not love its skys so filled with movement, its nights with the skys being lit by the beams of lighthouses? How can one not be sensitive to the light and to the countrysides which inspired the painters of Pont-Aven and Pouldu, Gaugin, Sérusier, Denis? The

Les Rochers (Ille et Vilaine)

Vitré (Ille et Vilaine)

TOUTES DIRECTIONS

SAINT-SERVAN

GARE MARITIME

Vedettes Hydroglisseurs

Centre Administratif

Morgat (Finistère)

proud breton cities, Vitré, Dinan, Locronan, Morlaix, Quimper...have all kept their medival houses often in skew-whiff. At the bottom of the steeples of the belltowers in toothed stones, the narrow streets of cobblestone wind round. On the bank, rivers look over the old washing places like the one in Vannes on the streams of Rohan.

Humble farms lined with small drystone walls conceal charming rustic furnishings, sculpted boxes, beds, buffets and dish cupboards.

Manors made with heavy stones of granite tell of the respect the manor-owner had. There is the abode of Madame de Sévigné of the Rochers, near Vitré. La Bourbansais around the Dinan area, Trécesson, Kerouartz, Kerjean, Caradeuc...They are still and especially these great

fortresses, a memory often intact of the wars which ravaged the province: Fougères, Vitré, Josselin, Combourg, Suscinio, Elven, Pontivy, the Solidor tower in Saint-Servan, Saint-Malo, the Latte fort.

Page to right:

Upper:
Caradeuc-Bécherej (Ille et Vilaine)

Lower:
Landéan (Ille et Vilaine)

Pages 56, 57
Saint-Malo (Ille et Vilaine)

Commana (Finistère)

The people here have beauty, the roughness of the countryside also. If the men no longer wear the felt-ribboned hat and the braided waistcoat, if the women have all but renounced the satin and velour garb and the hairstyles: the gogerin, with lace fittings, they haven't betrayed their roots. In the feasts as in the ceremonies, the young girls don't look distainfully on wearing the hairstyles of their grandmothers, the one in Fouesnant, in Quimper, Plougastel or Bigouden, a scaffolding of lace thirty meters high. The celtic circles assemble the young people in love with dance, music, and traditional costumes. The celtic harp is appreciated, the ringers have taken up again their bombarding practices, the heirs of the bards, Alain Stivell, Glenmor, Tri Yann, Servat and others, sing of the eternal Brittany:

Here we are proud
On the mont, on the sea,
In the face of storm,
The face of the tempests
By land and on the ocean,
We hold up our heads high.

Gilles Servat.

Saint-Pol de Léon - Kreizker (Finistère)

The people here will be your friend if you like to drink a sip of cider, to eat crêpes and waffles, andouille sausage of Guéméné, the lobster in the Amorican style, sea food and river fish, and the famous far for dessert. Bretons are lovers of fine tastes, but this is not the most important. The cuisine, the coffee, are only pretexts to for their goal: friendship. These people are my friends.

Locronan (Finistère)

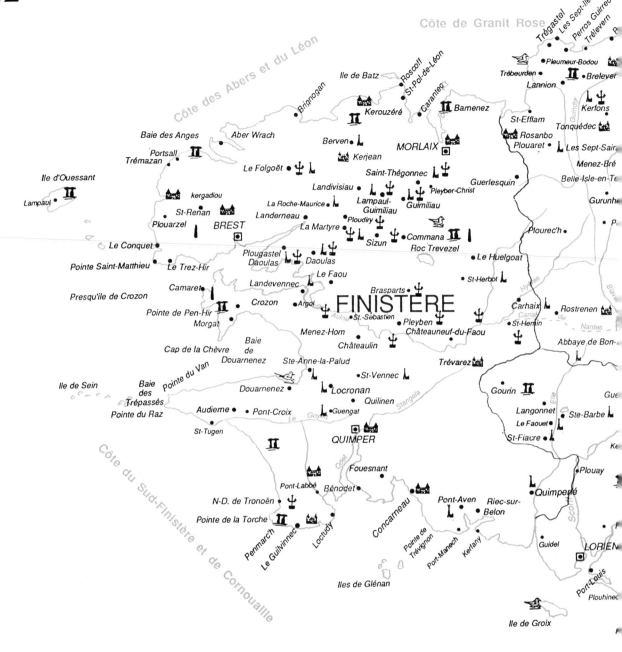

62

Castle - Castelli - Burg

Megaliths - Megaliti - Megalithen

Church - Chiesa - Kirche

Calvary - Calvario - Kalvarienberg

Sea Bird' reserve - Riserva Naturale - Naturreservat (meeresvögel)

50 KM

Côte d'Emeraude

Baie de Saint-Brieuc

Île de Bréhat
L'Arcouest
Paimpol
trieux
Lanloup
Plouha
St-Quay
Portrieux
Plérin-les-Rosaires
aria An Isquit
Lanvollon
âtelaudren
ST-BRIEUC
Hillion
Lamballe
Quintin
Moncontour
N-D du Haut
Abbaye de Boquen

Erquy
Sables-d'Or-les-Pins
Cap Fréhel
St-Cast
Le Val-André

Plancoët
Corseul
Pléven
La Hunaudaye
Jugon-les-Lacs
Lac de Jugon
La Bourbansais

COTES-
D'ARMOR
Lac de Guerlédan
Mur-de-Bretagne
Loudéac
Ste-Noyale
Pontivy

Pointe de La Garde-Guérin
Pointe du grouin
Cancale
ST-MALO
DINARD
Barrage
de la Rance
Mont Dol
Dol-de-Bretagne
Combourg
Tressé
DINAN

Mont St-Michel
Pontorson
Louvigné du Désert
Landal
Bonne-Fontaine
Landéan
Bazouges-la-Pérouse
Lanrigan
FOUGERES

Bécherel
Caradeuc
Montmuran
Montauban
ILLE-

St-Aubin du Cormier
St-Sulpice-la-Forêt

Comper
Paimpont
Forêt de Paimpont
Coëtquidan-St-Cyr

ET-
RENNES
Châteaugiron
VILAINE

Vilaine
VITRE
Les Rochers
Seiche
La Roche-aux-Fées
Rannée
La Guerche
de Bretagne

Abbaye N-D de Timadeuc
St-Nicodème
Josselin
Ploërmel
Guéhenno
Lizio
Malestroit
Callac
St-Marcel
La Gacilly
L'île aux Pies

MORBIHAN
Brech
Ste-Anne
d'Auray
Tours d'Elven
St-Avé
Rochefort-
en-Terre
uray
VANNES
Ploemel
Plessis-Josso
Questembert
Île aux Moines
Sarzeau
manéquer
Port-Navalo
Arzon Le Crouesty
Presqu'île de Rhuys
Suscinio
Ile d'Houat
Penestin
La Roche-
Bernard

Guipry Messac
St-Just

Redon

Semmon

Châteaubriand

Motte-Glain

LOIRE-
Canal de
Nantes
à Blain

Ile Hoedic
Côtes d'Amour
Le Croisic
La Baule
Pornichet
Pointe St-Gildas

Guérande
St-Nazaire
St-Joachim
St-Brévin-les-Pins
St-Brévin-l'Océan
Pornic

ATLANTIQUE
Brest

La Chapelle St-Sauver
Ancenis

NANTES
Haute-Goulaine
Vallet

Lac de Grand-Lieu

Clisson

Saint-Goazec - Castel Ruffel
(Finistère)

© 1992, Éditions Jean-Paul Gisserot.
Ce livre a été imprimé et façonné par Pollina à Luçon, 85400 - n° 15050. La couverture a été imprimée par Raynard, 35130 La Guerche de Bretagne, et pelliculée par Pollina à Luçon.